Letters to Michael

JANA &

ALSTON NOVAK

DEDICATION

To a kind and loving man who has always been generous with his time and
knowledge, always opening his home to all who wished to enter.
You have been a wonderful father, grandfather, and mentor to so many
people, and touched even more with your intellect and wisdom.
This book stands as a small thank you from a sample of the many lives you
have touched in your 80 years of living.
May you keep making a difference in the world!

ACKNOWLEDGMENTS

With gratitude to all those who took the time to share their thoughts and
love through these letters and notes.
Without you, this project would not have been possible.

A Father's Lessons: On Michael Novak on His 80th Birthday
Speech given at his birthday celebration

My father has taught me many things over the years. Lessons that have stuck with me despite the time that has passed and the distance geographically between us now. Indeed, one of those lessons is from decades ago – and is perhaps most appropriate for this evening...

One of the things my father taught me was that, as a child, one should be seen and not heard. You all know the classic saying, I am sure.

Apparently, I took this to heart – not surprisingly. I am my father's daughter after all. For there is a story of one dinner party my parents hosted, where I came downstairs repeatedly, each time in a different outfit. I then proceeded to – silently, of course – twirl about, show my clothes off, and – still completely silently – acknowledge my audience before disappearing upstairs again.

Twirl, acknowledge, repeat.

Letter of the law though: I was seen and not heard. And even my father, taskmaster and disciplinarian that he was, had to admit as much - much to his chagrin!

Well, tonight no costume changes are necessary, as I will be heard, as well as seen. Though my father might wish the opposite were still true!

As, in celebration of my father's 80 years on this earth, I will share with all of you a few of the many things my father has taught me.

Such as....

That God made Notre Dame "number one", and also, somewhat contradictory, yet still accurate, that God may not care who wins or loses, but His Mother sure does.

That questioning and curiosity are virtues – unless I'm questioning him too much.

That there is a talent and positive aspect to having determination, and even hard-headedness, but that it is a fine line that is not always best to cross....

And that it is a "Novak trait" to cross that line.

That criticism – <ahem> scholarly feedback is I think how he'd prefer it noted – is an integral part to growth and development, except when the tables are turned.
After all, I'm sure most of you have heard his lament about our first book together, and that my "scholarly feedback" was instead the "heartbreaking loss" of page after page of "the most beautiful prose ever"....

That sports are our religion, our sustenance, and our glory. Alabama's victory notwithstanding.

That humor should be practiced regularly and implemented frequently. A day lacking laughter is a day lacking value.

That high standards, ethics and honor are what make us who we are. Without them, we are nothing.

Of course, he plagiarized this from his father, but who's counting?!

That charm will actually get you everywhere. As will feigning helplessness.

That passion – for work, for others – is the key to a life well-lived and well-loved....

~

When I look at my father, I see a man who has taught me so much.

A scholar who emphasized questioning, challenging, learning. A professor who emphasized constant education. A sportsman who emphasized the pursuit of happiness in playing or watching athletic endeavors. A zealot who emphasized that God – or at least His Mother – made Notre Dame the best. A believer who emphasized faith, even when his team got rolled.

A witty man who emphasized being quick with a joke and even quicker with a laugh. An honorable man who emphasized that doing right is not a matter of who is watching. An ethical man who emphasized painting the underside of the stool despite the fact no one sees it. A gentle man who emphasized kindness and compassion. A tough man who emphasized never backing down from a fight, nor from high standards. An intense man who emphasized dedication to one's work, one's passion, one's love. A loving man who emphasized the many terms for love in Latin, and strove to achieve them all regularly.

A charming man who could woo a critic, a stewardess, and an audience equally. A talented man who could compete against the best of them. A generous man who never failed to share the spotlight....

~

As one of the many recipients of that spotlight here tonight, I should highlight this simple fact: The public Michael Novak is the same as the private Michael Novak – and all of us are blessed that this is true. As it means all of us can and should learn from him and his example.

So... Thank you dad, for being such an incredible role model and inspiration – to me and to so many people.... Thank you – and Happy Birthday!

Jana Miller
Daughter

To Michael Novak
With best wishes,
Ronald Reagan

Michael,

You and a very few other conservative intellectuals held the fort in the public square until reinforcements arrived. I remember slowly reading your columns in the old *Washington Star* (slowly so I could savor them), and how impressed I was by the power of your moral arguments and the depth of your thinking.

You unashamedly and powerfully applied Catholic teaching and biblical authority to the contemporary culture. That helped shape my own views and approach as I began to write a column of my own in 1984.

Michael, you are a gentleman of the first order and in the classical tradition of that word. You are full of kindness, wisdom, and truth. Your work and life will stand as a model and inspiration, not only to your contemporaries, but to those who follow you.

Happy 80th Birthday and many more, and may God continue to bless, protect and encourage you.

Cal Thomas,
Friend
Syndicated and USA Today Columnist/Fox News
Contributor

Dearest Michael,

What a triumph your life has been and how lucky Stanley and I are to count you among our dearest friends. I am grateful to *National Review*, Bill Buckley and John O'Sullivan for introducing us many years ago, and for the good, quality times we have shared together.

Whenever I introduced you as a speaker – when I chaired the National Review Institute or GOPAC meetings – I used to say that you were "so full of grace" that I always wished I was a Roman Catholic! When we travelled together in Israel, our appreciation of the country was hugely enhanced by your being with us. Your commentary and insight made every experience more vivid and meaningful.

In the summer of 2000, when Sir Denis and Lady Thatcher visited us in Vail, the only two men I invited to come and stay were you and Rush Limbaugh. I remember Margaret telling me how much she esteemed your writing and how very much she learned from your fabulous book, *The Spirit of Democratic Capitalism*! She studied it!

We had so much fun in Vail and she reminded me that it is important in life to keep company with "people of like mind!"

Your wonderful book that you wrote together with Jana, *Tell Me Why*, is one of my "turn to" books when I need answers or am sad or in doubt. It helped me when we lost our son Stanley and was something I turned to frequently when I was hurting and angry, for understanding... Of course the book, *Washington's God*, that you wrote when I was Regent at Mount Vernon and dedicated to me, meant the world to me and I will forever be grateful for your generosity.

Your life has been one of scholarship and excellence. You have continually done work worth doing and at the same time kept a sense of balance, humor, and love of family.

Happy, happy 80th Birthday and I really mean it when I say, Stanley and I hope there are many more times we will share together.

With high regard and love in abundance,

Gay and Stanley

Gay Hart Gaines, Friend
Former Regent, Mount Vernon Ladies Association

ARCHDIOCESE OF WASHINGTON
5001 Eastern Avenue
Post Office Box 29260
Washington, D.C. 20017

Office of the Archbishop

June 20, 2013

Dear Mr. Novak,

It has come to my attention that on September 9, 2013 you will celebrate your 80th birthday. On this happy occasion, I would like to join my personal congratulations to those of your family and many friends.

When you look back over your life, I suspect that you count many blessings not the least of which are your family and your faith. For those of us who admire your intellectual acumen and dedication to the ongoing challenge of the engagement of the wisdom of God with culture today, I hope you would count our esteem and appreciation as marks, as well, of your accomplishments.

For so many enduring signs of His goodness and love, I join you in offering thanks to God and ask that God continue to bless you who have been such a blessing to so many in these past eight decades.

With every personal good wish, I am

Faithfully in Christ,

Archbishop of Washington

Dear Mr. Novak,

It has come to my attention that on September 9, 2013, you will celebrate your 80th birthday. On this happy occasion, I would like to join my personal congratulations to those of your family and many friends.

When you look back over your life, I suspect that you count many blessings not the least of which are your family and your faith. For those of us who admire your intellectual acumen and dedication to the ongoing challenge of the engagement of the wisdom of God with culture today, I hope you would count our esteem and appreciation as marks of your accomplishments as well.

For so many enduring signs of His goodness and love, I join you in offering thanks to God and ask that God continue to bless you who have been such a blessing to so many in these past eight decades.

With every personal good wish, I am

Faithfully in Christ,

Donald Cardinal Wuerl
Archbishop of Washington

Michael, in celebrating your remarkable eighty years, I shall leave
to others the praise of your extraordinary accomplishments,
because it is as a loving husband to Karen, father to Jana, Tanya,
and Richard, and brother to Ben and Mary Ann that I know you
best.

Of all the occasions, both formal and casual, which we have
celebrated, it is those dinners at the table of the Novaks during
Karen's last two years that I treasure. There you were at the head
of the table, very much the *pater familias*, tender and solicitous of
your bride, directing good friends by some mysterious logic to
their seats, and Karen at the long end of the table nearest the
kitchen, still wearing her apron, listening for the sound that would
alert her to something in the kitchen that needed attention while
carrying on a lively conversation about Rilke!

The table, laden with the food one can only dream of, was
miraculous, and it is the memory of those evenings, where in the
candlelight the conversation flowed and the warmth of family and
friendship filled the room, that will endure in my memory and
where I shall always see you.

> *Susannah Patton*
> *Friend*

Dear Michael,

I am delighted to share remembering and honoring your 80th.
There are so many ways I appreciate and value your friendship.

You, your life, your great body of work, gave new depths and
paths to our spiritual lives. This will always be a valued gift to us
all.

I am thankful for one special gift. When Ernie died, and I was living alone, you and Karen quietly reached out. No fanfare. You were both just there, including me in dinners, an evening out, and being with friends. That beautiful, extension of help and friendship is a gift I will always keep in my heart.

May this day, and all the years ahead, be blessed.

Please know that my prayers and friendship will be there.

> *Margaret Lefever*
> *Friend*

My affection for Michael is exceeded only by my admiration for the wonderful work he has done since his historic break with the Left about 45 years ago.

> *Norman Podhoretz*
> *Friend*
> *Founding neoconservative*
> *Writer, Commentary magazine*

I knew Ben before I came to know Michael, but I knew from the start there was something special about the Novaks. It's been a real pleasure of my life over the past year coming to know and work with Michael, and experiencing Ave Maria, the special town he has helped to forge.

In one visit in September 2012, I brought a girlfriend from Penn State. I wanted her to meet the Novak brothers – they were special, I told her. After a visit of a few days, I sat out with her one night by the pool after Ben and Michael had gone to bed. She was being unusually quiet, so I asked her if she was all right. "I just keep asking myself," she started to say uncertainly, "if all of this is real." What did she mean? "Michael is the kindest, sweetest man I think I've ever met. I've been treated like part of the family, and he just met me. We ate a real dinner tonight at the table, like a family. I haven't had dinner at the table with my own family – ever. Men in this town, and especially Michael and Ben are true gentlemen, and I didn't think there ever really were any. Michael has shown me what a man is really like, in just a few days. That's why I'm being quiet –being it all seems fantastically unreal, but it's real."

Hope this isn't too sappy, but it's a true story.

Tom Shakely
Friend
Assistant to Michael and Ben

Dear Michael,

My memories with you date way back to those wonderful Super Bowl days when Judy and I would sit with you and Karen and discuss the current game, or what projects we were currently pursuing, or how the world could be a better place and what we were doing about it. I noticed we almost always sat together no matter where our Jack Kemp assigned seats were located.

I also remember what an honor it was to have you and Karen included with our first guests for dinner at our "new" home, Moss Neck. Frank O'Reilly literally wrote the book on the Battle of Fredericksburg and explained the Stonewall connection in copious detail. (He is still doing it for the National Park Service about three times a year. Last year he lectured from our front porch to over 200 citizens from all over the country in his "Sunset at Moss Neck" event.) Brit and Kim Hume discussed their current political projects at Fox News. They would be doing the same if the dinner was held this evening, only with more gusto. Lon and Brenda Solomon told of their daughter's sad plight in being born with severe mental deficiencies. They have formed a support organization in their church to help parents with the same problems trying to live a normal life while providing care for their severely disadvantaged children. You and Karen provided the moral glue that was omnipresent in all of the discussions. We cherished your presence and comments. As you can see, I still have a pretty good memory of the evening (for an old man).

There was a recent article in the WSJ about age 80 becoming the new 60. With you, I'm sure it's true. In fact, your thoughts and philosophy of life are too eternal to be categorized. And that's why we love you. May you have a very happy birthday--and many more to follow. There's still much left to do on Earth.

Love and best wishes,

> *Gil Shelton*
> *Friend*
> *Commission Member, Virginia Governor's Commission*
> *on Government Reform & Restructuring*
> *Husband of Judy Shelton*

Here are some of our most treasured moments with Michael:

Savoring Italian sausage while sharing "the joy of sports" at Camden Yards, RFK Stadium, and FedEx Field.

Joining in the simple summer pleasures with friends and family at "Templeton House" in Lewes: eating corn - while Michael tells corny rabbi-priest jokes, witnessing the bizarre mating ritual of horseshoe crabs spawning on the beaches of Delaware Bay, engaging in lively discussions on topics such as Kierkegaard or whether cats have free will.

Michael and Karen serving as Godparents for our son Henry.

Hearing Michael discuss the American Founding, *Centesimus Annus* and *The Spirit of Democratic Capitalism*, international human rights and religious freedom; his mind always soaring on the two wings of faith and reason, even while part of him is grounded in his beloved birthplace of Johnstown.

Sparkling dinners at Northampton Street with Richard and Jana, church leaders from Poland, and Karen's awe-inspiring angels.

Seeing in Michael's adoration for and companionship with Karen a model for our own marriage.

> *Adam and Nina*
> *Friends*
>
> *Adam Meyerson*
> *President, The Philanthropy Roundtable*
>
> *Nina Shea*
> *Director, Center for Religious Freedom, Hudson Institute*

Reflections on our brother Michael Novak on his 80th Birthday

As far as his siblings could tell, Michael was clearly the SUN and THE son from the moment he was born. We knew he was our Mother's favorite even before she sheepishly admitted it not long before her death, when we all burst out laughing because it was so obvious. Our parents adored him, and came to listen closely to his thoughts from a young age. All of the four succeeding children -- Richard two years younger, Jim six years younger, Ben ten years younger, and Mary Ann 15 years younger -- looked up to Michael naturally, and emulated our parents in listening to his judgment.

Older brothers usually have standing in their family but Michael was both eldest and *in loco parentis*, whether we liked it or not. Even before his many awards and celebrated writings, he provided the framework and set the tone for our family life, providing most of the books we read growing up and developing our love of literature. He has been the lodestar of our family, a towering intellect, the guide to our Catholic faith that no school or parish church could compete with, our global travel advisor, our guide to our Slovak heritage, our political arbiter, our language coach, our football sportscaster, making it a distinctly difficult task to hew a markedly different path in the major institutions of life.

He leads us still as we struggle to understand Richard's death in 1964, just as he led as we buried our parents in 1992 and 1993, followed shortly by our brother Jim's untimely death in 1996. We share his love for Karen, and mourned with him as she too left us behind in this vale of tears.

We have broken bread together in far-flung locales such as Slovakia, Krakow, Rome, London, and at our homes in Washington, DC and Florida, sharing most Thanksgiving, Christmas, and Easter meals, regular birthday celebrations, and many, many special evenings with family and close friends. We have toasted each other and boasted of our ties, and when lines went down between us, we drank gallons and gallons of Manhattans, superb wine, and dark beers and argued it out, loudly or united in silence.

We have been inspired and guided by Michael's brilliance and his astounding successes, by his genuine kindness and generosity to us, and we are still circling in his firmament.

In this, his 80th year, we salute our dearly beloved eldest sibling, and pledge to him our enduring loyalty and love, in the Novak tradition,

Na zdravie!

> *Ben and Mary Ann Novak*
> *Brother and Sister*

Dear Michael,

The first time I met you was at Eileen's and my newlywed reception in Johnstown soon after our wedding in 1980. From the beginning you've helped make me feel part of the family. I've always appreciated your strong commitment to our extended Novak-Sakmar-Atwood family and truly feel a cousin to you.

For our wedding you had mailed us a copy of *Guns of Latimer* in which you inscribed "on the wedding day of yet another generation!" I did read the book some years later. This rather sheltered WASP-y boy found your description of Slavs on pages xv-xvi very enlightening. Recently, Eileen and I celebrated our 33rd wedding anniversary. I am so blessed to have married this excellent Slovak woman!

At that reception and other times I was excited to share with you how I had studied *Spirit of Democratic Capitalism* in graduate school at what was then CBN University, now Regent University, where I received my MBA and my MA in Public Policy. Your book has had a profound influence on my worldview and thinking. To this day I am still citing it, as recently as in a major gift proposal I wrote for IRD last year. The book is packed full of faith and reason, and the product of a great deal of hard work, in which you persevered diligently with a servant's heart.

I remember when Eileen and I had the privilege of joining you in London for the celebration of your Templeton Prize. At the dinner at AEI, I had the opportunity to say something congratulatory to you. I did not think you would willingly receive a compliment for wisdom or brilliance because you know that such things are gifts from God. So I simply said, "You've worked very hard" and I had the sense that it was the best compliment I could give you. You were able to receive recognition for your obedience and diligence, but too humble to accept credit for being God's instrument in revealing truth.

You have my gratitude also for a far less weighty matter, but one that has contributed significantly to my enjoyment in life nevertheless – namely, you are the one who introduced me to Manhattans. It has become my most favorite "adult beverage" and I almost never even consider other options any more, when the ingredients of this ambrosial libation are available. I hope I have the opportunity to mix one for you soon and toast "to your continued good health and prosperity!"

Blessings and love,

Tom Atwood
Cousin Eileen's husband

Michael,

Happy 80th birthday! Nothing I can write is adequate to honor the moment. You have touched so many people – the learned and the ignorant, the powerful and the helpless, the saintly and the despicable. We thank Providence for you, a much respected and much loved man!

Elizabeth Shaw
Assistant to Michael Novak
Adjunct Professor of Philosophy, Catholic University

Stonehill was small, only six years old, when I came to it from Donegal in 1954. Since I was a candidate for admission to the Holy Cross Fathers (we were called postulants), I lived in Donahue Hall, the Big House on the Hill. There was another group of "professed" religious who lived at St. Pius X Seminary near the old Ames Airport, to the south and west of us. We were not allowed to mingle with them. Michael Novak and his brother Richard, of beloved memory, were among those who lived at Pius X. We were once invited by the "professed" seminarians to a soiree (sic) and smoked some of their rolled cigarettes. They greeted all of us warmly. Of course, we admired them greatly for they had been through the dreaded "novitiate."

Sports were few, and self-organized. There was touch football, played by a group of intramural teams on fall afternoons. Pius X, quickly dubbed "The Sem," fielded a football team of professed religious. I was new to everything American, but touch football was not that hard to analyze. We (the postulants) felt it incumbent on us to cheer for our older brothers. And so we did. When the quarterback threw there was a player on the Sem team who frequently went up for the ball, and came down with it. His name was Michael Novak. Looking back, I could not say that he was the tallest or the fastest – but there was a mixture of grit and huskiness that made him the terror of the Stonehill football field.

Michael went to the Gregorian in Rome, and we headed for the dreaded Novitiate where we were *novices* not novitiates. A boot camp in spirituality some call it. It was, well, spiritual after a fashion. We recited the Hours of the BVM, did kitchen-work, collected apples in the afternoon, ate apple pies at suppertime, and in general kept our eyes averted. And, kept quiet. The Grand Silence was from the end of night-prayer till the morning bell. It was a perfect time for the more worldly novices "*to act the maggot.*" Irish phrase: guess at that one!

Michael spent two years in Rome, I understand, and then returned to Holy Cross College in Washington, D.C. where he parted ways with the Congregation of Holy Cross and went on to Harvard. It was there that he ran into the brazen ethnics *who defined truth for the rest of us.* Michael found a species of ethnic that was unmeltable and he was *numero uno.*

Next time I saw Michael, he was behind a typewriter thumping out a dispatch for some American Journal. A mundane Pope, named John XXIII, had called an Ecumenical or Universal Council, called Vatican II, and the whole world seemed to be there. It must have been manna for a mind like the one that Michael had, and there was fodder for rethinking the whole Catholic Church – even God is said to have complained at being rethought – after Eden, and Egypt and all that, not to mention the Incarnation and the way John of the Cross made poetry out of it. The Council lasted five years and we are the results of it. I call it and us "empirical residue," just to make the point that the Holy Spirit can have fun too.

The Washington years are too long to chronicle, but after teaching in many Universities, Michael became a Fellow of the American Enterprise Institute and I became President of my alma mater and his, Stonehill College. It was a pleasure to have Michael back to campus so often as Trustee or lecturer in the place he saw grow from a seedling. It was a crowning pleasure to be with him in London to see him receive the Templeton Award, and to meet Sir John Templeton and Lady Thatcher and all those who supported him for the award. He sent me back across the ocean next day with $200,000 in my pocket for the Novak Scholarship before the Brits took their taxes off the top.

Happy Birthday, Michael, I hope you are still thinking ahead of the brazen ethnics!

> *Fr. Bartley MacPhaidin, CSC*
> *Friend*
> *President Emeritus, Stonehill College*

It was in 1953 and I was living at home with my parents, Michael's Aunt Helen and Uncle John Sakmar. 1953 was, for me, a very special year in that I would be graduating from college with a Baccalaureate degree in Nursing, and in November, would be marrying Keith, the man who would be my husband and with whom I was so in love.

My parents lived in a modest but well maintained three-family home in the city of New Britain, Connecticut. We lived on Wilcox Street, which was pretty much lined with three family homes and a Slovak Catholic Church, Rectory and neat, green grounds. Almost every household was Slovak, and most were members of that church. Hardly anyone had cars so there was very little traffic on our street.

Because we, too, never owned a car we did not go anywhere! When my father was on vacation that meant he had more time to tend to his very productive gardens and fruit trees in our back yard. This is why we were so happy to have the next generation in our extended Sakmar family come to visit us. It began when cousin Charlie Sakmar drove his wife, children, and/or parents from Stamford, Connecticut. This was very exciting for us and we enjoyed their visits. Another favorite carful of visitors were the Novaks who were either on their way to, or returning from, Stonehill College where their eldest sons, Michael and Richard, were students and seminarians. It was through these visits that I got to know my Uncles Ben and Kasian and their families.

Michael tells me that, on one particular weekend that summer in 1953, his parents picked him up at Stonehill, and on their return to Johnstown, they would be stopping in Connecticut to visit Uncle John and Aunt Helen and family. Years later, Michael confessed to me that he did not want to stop because he thought it would be boring sitting around and talking to middle aged cousins who looked like they ate "too much kapusta and perogi" and just sat around and talked. Typical twenty year old, wouldn't you say? And he was in the seminary! Well, that day he found out that he had girl cousins who ate Slovak food that had not yet destroyed their waistlines, and who talked about things that were interesting to him!

On that lovely summer day in my father's back yard, while the rest of the family "sat around and talked," Michael and I found a quiet spot under the grapevine and discussed school. Both of us were attending Catholic Colleges and we compared our studies, more specifically, St. Thomas Aquinas. Today, I couldn't tell you today very much about Thomas or what exactly about him fascinated us both so much, but, for me, the conversation was stimulating and delightful. It was also very refreshing to learn that this young, pious and intelligent young man was my cousin. I thought... "he is going to amount to something." That meeting under the grapevine also established a lifelong relationship that exists today.

Happy birthday with much cousin love, Mike!

> *Fran Casey*
> *Cousin*
> *Daughter of John Sakmar, brother to Ben Sakmar*

I often think about the war games that we played on Saturdays. I remember how I would get up early in the morning to walk from Virginia Avenue to Arlington St. When I arrived there Michael and Richard would have hundreds of toy soldiers all over the floor. They were ready to be divided up among the three of us. I never saw so many soldiers as were on that floor. Jeeps, tanks, army trucks were all lined up ready for war.

It was always sad to have to walk back home after a wonderful day of playing war. I hope you have a great birthday, Michael and many more.

Your cousin, private Larry reporting

> *Larry Novak*
> *Cousin*
> *3rd son of John Novak, the brother of Michael J. Novak*

Tribute to Michael Novak for 80th birthday:

In the Gospel of St. John, chapter 17, Jesus prays his great priestly prayer before he goes back to the Father. He prays thus: "Consecrate them in the truth, your word is truth. As you sent me into the word, so I send them into the world, and I consecrate myself for them, so that they may be consecrated in the truth. I pray not only for them, but also for those who believe in me through their word . . ."

My cousin, Michael Novak, fulfilling the example of his father, truly was dedicated to the truth. He allowed the Holy Spirit to guide him to the Truth. His entire life was led by the Spirit of Truth. He allowed the Holy Spirit to lead him. God chose him to be consecrated to the truth, and thereby to be consecrated to the Holy Spirit.

Our world desperately needs more people like Michael Novak, people who are consecrated to the Holy Spirit and to the One Truth, which has as its source the Triune God, Father, Son, and Holy Spirit. I praise and thank God for the wondrous gifts that he has bestowed on him, gifts that he has used and still continues to use for the greater honor and glory of God.

> *Rev. Andrew C. Stanko, VF*
> *Cousin*
> *Son of Andrew Stanko, cousin of Michael J. Novak*

Dear Michael,

Jenny joins me in wishing you a very happy birthday. We are so very grateful for your friendship over so many years and very thankful for the influence your life and work has had on our lives. So we wish you every blessing on your 80th birthday and wish you many more to come. You have touched many lives and we are thankful for how your friendship has touched ours.

Please stay in touch.

Michael and Jenny Cromartie
Friends
Vice President, Ethics and Public Policy Institute

I am so grateful for the thoughtfulness of Michael Novak. His kindness and sincerity have always been apparent and these are valuable traits, but the world needs great thinking clearly communicated. Michael delivers. There are so many thoughts going on in Michael's mind, we can understand when sometimes it seems as if he isn't present in the physical realm. Some call it absent mindedness. It doesn't bother me.

Without Michael and his writing, I would not have the wellspring of inspired thinking that helps clarify so many of the principles in which I deeply believe but don't always describe clearly or succinctly.

Thank God for Michael Novak and his thoughtfulness.

> *Jimmy Kemp*
> *Friend*
> *President, Jack Kemp Foundation*

Always willing to buck the politically correct, Professor Michael Novak has been a faithful, knowledgeable, and creative Catholic scholar. Serious Catholic intellectuals owe him a profound debt of gratitude for his varied, numerous, and substantial career accomplishments.

> *Joseph A. Varacalli, Ph.D.*
> *Friend*
> *S.U.N.Y. Distinguished Service Professor*
> *Co-Founder, Society of Catholic Social Scientists,*
> *Board of Directors Member, Fellowship of Catholic Scholars*
> *Director, Nassau Community College-S.U.N.Y. Center for Catholic Studies*

His reputation cowers me
Before I meet him.
His goodness showers me
When I meet him.

Michael of passionate otherness.

He takes me on to book keep
His finances chez Novak,
Ensuring I fall not asleep
Midst his voluminous tomes stack to stack.

As time passes, I note more
Of this thinker extraordinaire.
To all who come to his door,
He is kind and gentle, firm and fair.

He treasures Karen, his "Irradiant Soul,"
The one who complements him fully.
He loves her without measure and whole,
For she is his happiness truly.

He lets Karen go to God
With faith so tested and true.
He has this road before trod
And strength from Him drew.

Beyond telling, I remain amazed
At Michael's humble heart,
His fervor for truth ablaze,
His befriending this simple upstart.

Michael of passionate otherness.

Thank you for sterling example,
Thank you for friendship unbound,
Thank you for love steadfast and ample.
Thank God for keeping you around.

Happy 80th!
Love,
Suzanne

Suzanne Shaffer
Friend

Dear Michael,

When I think of you, I picture you smiling that wonderful broad smile of yours that puts a twinkle in your eyes. It is a look that is very welcoming and engaging at the same time. Over the years, I have often heard you speak both in public and in private with family members present, and have always enjoyed hearing your perspective on the topic at hand. You have a way of bringing extra insight and relevance into many of your stories – many are vignettes of human experience, which you frequently relate to your hometown memories of growing up in Johnstown, PA – which is so endearing.

I know how much both Tom and I, and frankly all who were present, thoroughly enjoyed your commemorative talk at IRD several years ago, honoring Diane Knippers. It was with joy and anticipation of hearing one of your talks that Tom and I relished attending numerous events in DC. Also, the dinners and gatherings we had at your home in Washington over the years with family and friends were a great treat: seeing Karen and Mary Ann cooking delectable dishes and you offering welcomed beverages. And we loved how you engaged our son, Christopher when he was younger, in discussions while we were visiting with you. I clearly remember your commenting once on his name. You said it meant he was a "Christ – bearer" and defined the significance of what that meant. It was an uplifting moment for him and for us, as we listened.

The invitation you offered, encouraging us to join you, Karen and the family in London, England upon the occasion of your receiving the prestigious John Templeton Prize for Progress in Religion in the mid-nineties was an experience Tom and I will always remember with great fondness and pride. Everyone present in Westminster Abbey was so delighted as Madame Thatcher spoke glowingly of you and your accomplishments along with other dignitaries who presented you this distinguished award. I can still picture that amazing, memorable scene and the fabulous festivities we attended while we were there celebrating with you and family. It was a storybook moment in time. I know how very proud your parents would have been had they been there to see you receive this honor.

Another special event we attended that was truly lovely was when you and Karen celebrated your 40th Wedding Anniversary at the Army Navy Club. The two of you – wedded soul mates – were a joy to behold. Everyone toasted to your happiness! We've attached a few photos for your remembrance and enjoyment. Attending Richard and Lucy's beautiful wedding was another memorable event for us. Also, Tom and I appreciated your thoughtful wedding gift to us, your book, *Guns of Latimer*, which we both took pleasure in reading. And we haven't stopped reading many of the extraordinary books and articles that you have penned over the years. We are especially looking forward to reading your latest, *Writing from Left to Right*, real soon.

Recalling our numerous Sakmar/Novak gatherings in Johnstown throughout the years brings an abundance of warm memories of home-cooked Slovak food, laughter and books. The Novak male cousins, amazingly, always brought along huge volumes tucked under their arms, either to deflect from the typical heightened conversations swirling around and/or escape from the boredom that accompanies teens sometimes. Although, gladly devouring any one of my mother's, their Aunt Fran's, homemade desserts – whether it be her fruit pies, cakes, gobs, rolls, or her famous nut and poppy seed rolls – would, undoubtedly, change things, and bring huge, satisfied grins to everyone's faces.

Speaking of my mother, I remember her telling me touching stories whenever we would reminisce about their early married years while living in St. Mary's, or in McKeesport, PA, where, as you know, my parents shared a home with yours for a while and where I was born. One of them was Mom saying how especially excited the Novak male cousins had been at my birth. She mentioned how much you all enjoyed the novelty of having the first baby girl relative to coo over instead of having just another boy. And she highlighted how caring you were, in particular…how nice is that! Following soon after, came the birth of your only sister, my dear cousin Mary Ann, which made for twice as much fun for everyone.

One of the more memorable times in Johnstown was in the fall of 2000 when you, Mary Ann, Ben and the Novak family (plus relatives, Mary Sue and Larry Boring) put together a fantastic Sakmar Family Reunion – 100th Year Remembrance in honor of our late Grandpa Benedict "Ben" Sakmar. He was one of several brothers to immigrate from Czechoslovakia as a young man at the turn of the century. It was meaningful to hear of his early life in Brutovce and how he came to America, and settled in Johnstown. It was heartwarming to see so many relatives come from across the states and share their memories of their families, as well as of Benedict, his wife Anna Timchak Sakmar and their three children. We loved watching the film that was shown of a wonderful trip to Brutovce, Slovakia taken earlier in the summer by the Novaks, Borings, and several others who recorded their travels and the great dinner party held in their honor while visiting with the Slovak Sakmar and Biroschak relatives. Tom and I both wished we could have been among those relatives who had made that historic trip. Fortunately, the Borings put together a huge book of photographs reflecting our heritage that we were able to buy copies of later. Our celebrating together that evening over a lovely dinner while toasting our forefathers with the traditional Slivovitz (a gift from cousin Ben), seeing photographs and watching the film; and then the next day taking part in a walking tour of Cambria City, visiting the beautiful, old churches there during their annual fall festival; going to "Pops Market" in Morrellville, where our grandparents lived and raised their children, and seeing the old graveyard nearby made for unforgettable memories. So were the stories that went with it all. We have much to treasure and much for which to be thankful.

Michael, "Here's to your good health!" and to your amazing, vibrant, fruitful life. Happy 80th Birthday! As your dad, and my Uncle Mickey, would always say, "Every day is Christmas!"

Much love and blessings,

> *Eileen Sakmar Atwood*
> *Cousin*
> *Daughter of Edward Sakmar, the youngest brother of Michael's mother Irene*

Michael,

Happy eightieth birthday! A great time to review a remarkable life. I would like to add a few personal notes.

I first encountered Michael and his work in the early 1980s.

The Cold War had reached a new intensity with the Soviet Union on offense in Nicaragua, El Salvador, Grenada and elsewhere. There was a substantial Liberation Theology movement shifting the Catholic Church toward support for insurgencies in the Third World. In Europe and America there was a growing anti-war, disarmament, nuclear freeze movement.

In this tense period Michael Novak was a breath of fresh air and his writing was a beacon of light.

As a young Congressman I found myself listening to him explain the theory of Just War. He brought to us a thorough understanding of Pope John Paul II's rejection of Liberation theology. Again and again Michael was the most influential intellectual helping us understand how to oppose Communism intellectually and how to show the fallacies of the disarmament movement.

When the Soviet Empire collapsed Michael turned his intellectual beliefs into a personal commitment to help the people of Poland by going every summer to teach young Poles about freedom, free enterprise and Catholic beliefs.

Michael's work to extend an understanding of freedom, capitalism and faith was aimed at Americans even more than Poles. His major books were extraordinarily influential in both legitimizing the moral basis of capitalism and in weaving together American liberty and American religious belief. Michael Novak's contributions have made many Americans understand better the historic and continuing role of God and religion in American public life.

As a colleague at the American Enterprise Institute, I found Michael's door always open, his mind always engaging and his spirit of enthusiasm and affection contagious.

He is one of the true quiet giants who made the last half century a victory for freedom.

Newt Gingrich
Friend
Former Speaker of the U.S. House of Representatives
President, The Gingrich Group

To Michael Novak
With Best Wishes,

Michael,

George and I have not known you as long as most of the people that will be celebrating with you today, nor have we spent as much time with you as they have been privileged to do. You and Karen came into our lives rather late in life and we are so grateful that we met through the friendship of our wonderful daughters.

No doubt there will many stories told today of your friendship with great political, spiritual and literary figures of our time. We have a deep respect for your talent and honesty and courage in standing up for what you believe is right, and for the influence you have had in the lives of people that direct the course of our churches, our country and even the world.

But the Michael we know is a grandfather that shared the joy of a family night at the baseball park with George – a generous friend that allowed us to share some family time at the beach house where we were so blessed to get to know your wonderful Karen – and the dinner companion that kept us laughing so much with stories and shared memories of Karen. You have been a wonderful mentor to our daughter Brenna – she values your advice and counsel, and we thank you so much for the love and kindness you have always shown her. She once told me that being with you and Karen was a "life adventure" and I am so glad that we have been able to share just a little bit of that adventure.

> *Happy Birthday from Texas!*
> *George and Judy Hapes*
> *Friends*
> *Parents of Jana's friend Brenna*

WILLIAM E. SIMON, JR.

June 6, 2013

Dear Michael:

Many happy returns on your 80th!

What a joy it is to reflect on all your friendship has meant to my Dad and me for over 30 years now. Beginning with the Lay Commission and right up to this present moment, you have been a source of wisdom, encouragement and inspiration to us both.

Writing *Living the Call* with you was one of the great experiences of my life, and I am honored and humbled to be able to say we are "co-authors". I learned so much from you over the years of discussion leading up to our collaboration: You have given me real insight into what it means to be a Catholic; you have challenged me to stretch my spiritual and intellectual muscles; and you have inspired me with the boldness of your faith and the courage with which you live it.

You are also one of the most truly optimistic people I know. To spend time with you (which I wish happened more often) is to feel that all will be right with this crazy world of ours, because it is God's world, and he is in control.

Happy 80th Birthday Michael! I will certainly raise a glass to you on September 9, and will ask Monsignor Torgerson to say a Mass of thanksgiving to celebrate the occasion.

With warmest wishes, as always,

Sincerely,

Bill

Happy Birthday Michael!

xo + o + o

44

Dear Michael,

Many happy returns on your 80th!

What a joy it is to reflect on all your friendship has meant to my Dad and me for over 30 years now. Beginning with the Lay Commission and right up to this present moment, you have been a source of wisdom, encouragement and inspiration to us both.

Writing *Living the Call* with you was one of the great experiences of my life, and I am honored and humbled to be able to say we are "co-authors." I learned so much from you over the years of discussion leading up to our collaboration: you have given me real insight into what it means to be a Catholic; you have challenged me to stretch my spiritual and intellectual muscles; and you have inspired me with the boldness of your faith and the courage with which you live it.

You are also one of the most truly optimistic people I know. To spend time with you (which I wish happened more often) is to feel that all will be right with this crazy world of ours, because it is God's world, and he is in control.

Happy 80th Birthday Michael! I will certainly raise a glass to you on September 9, and will ask Monsignor Torgerson to say a Mass of thanksgiving to celebrate the occasion.

With warmest wishes, as always,

> *Sincerely,*
> *Bill*
>
> *William E. Simon, Jr.*
> *Friend*
> *Co-founder, William E. Simon & Sons*
> *Co-chair, William E. Simon Foundation*

Dear Michael:

Joyous greetings on your eightieth Birthday…and many, many happy returns of the day.

You are a man of many flags…innovative intellectual, statesman, scholar, counselor to the nation's leadership, and novelist. But we wish to celebrate your gift of Friendship.

Our friendship with you was a planned event. Forty eight years ago this month, as we were settling ourselves into our new post as faculty residents at Stanford, we heard the news that Michael Novak, "the young guy who is challenging the Church to wake up and get with it," was coming to Stanford's theology department. It was hard to believe that Stanford, steeped as it was in staid Protestantism and soft-core secularism, was hiring a Catholic theologian, let alone an outspoken one and one with one of those old ethnic names. But Stanford had done it, and we set out to get to know you.

As faculty residents we were encouraged to regularly invite faculty members to mingle with our freshmen males and to somehow dilute their barbarism. Michael, you accepted the challenge, but little did we know that we'd get two for one. Along with you came the radiant Karen! And along with Karen came Richard in utero. You became an instant presence on the campus and you and Karen became permanent residents in our hearts. Do you remember how Marilyn modeled for some of Karen's early paintings?

We have stayed in touch over the years and over vast distances, often meeting and staying in one another's homes. Michael, you often promoted Kevin as a participant in a plush conference at Aspen or Washington. Meanwhile we read your books and followed your increasing influence within the Church and within our government. If truth be told, we dropped your name at every opportunity!

Michael, you have been so much a part of the sweetness in our lives. When we look at the map of our family life, there are little Novak flags all over it. You recommended Kevin to John Silber to head up a World Bank project in Portugal and that led us both back to Portugal, but then on to a new life in Boston. You helped Hilary get a Journalism fellowship in Washington, then a job at Crisis Magazine and then to a great job as Ed Feulner's speechwriter. That, in turn, led to her meeting her future husband, Jeff Tucker. And like the good friend you are, you always made the effort to come to Boston for our weddings. (Michael, if and when Justin finds the Karen in his life, he's expecting you to be there for him.)

Besides the important and thoughtful interventions in our lives, there has also been your personal example. We won't embarrass you by trotting out your many virtues, except to mention your joyous buoyancy. Slavs are supposed to be brooding and dark, but not you, Michael. A smile...a joke...a positive interruption of a disagreeable event is your "default position." Your ability to overcome darkness with Christian optimism has been for us one of the prime gifts of your friendship. And, yes, Michael, Notre Dame will come back this year and take the National Championship!

Michael, we regret we can't be with you to celebrate in person, but in honor of your 80th year, we'll turn toward Ave Maria and raise our very dry martinis in your direction.

And finally, Michael, keep all those flags flying…particularly that friendship flag. As Pooh answered his good friend, Piglet's question, "We'll be Friends Forever, won't we, Pooh?"

"Yes, Piglet. Even longer."

> *Kevin and Marilyn Ryan*
> *Friends*
> *Co-authors, column for* The Pilot, *a Catholic Archdiocesan Newspaper*

Michael,

Since I was 80 on May 31st, I am now an elder in your society and will be able to pontificate as I wish with no interruption or criticism from someone much younger.

As an elder, I am not so foolish as to attempt to dissect your literary and academic achievements (I defer to Kay for that task). However, I must note that I have particular fondness for your 400 page treatise, "The Spirit of Democratic Capitalism," that so dramatically influenced Pope John Paul II and Margaret Thatcher and changed the world for so many.

By "divine" circumstance, Kay and I were allowed to join you in London for your lecture at Westminster Abbey when you received the Templeton Award for Progress in Religion. It was indeed a most deserved award for all your achievements and we were honored to have the privilege to attend and be included with your family for the dinner at the Savoy that followed. It will forever be one of the fondest times of our lives.

Now, young man, since I have delegated to my younger wife the task of integrating your academic and literary achievements into this collection of tributes, I would like to talk a little about Michael Novak, the man, and my friend.

You may recall (at your advanced age) that I previously served as the Assistant Majority Leader of the Colorado House of Representatives and when you and I became acquainted I was a Regent of the University of Colorado, and subsequently Counselor to the Secretary of Health and Undersecretary of Health in the Reagan administration. In those roles I was involved in many public policy issues, which I shared with you from time to time to gain a broader perspective. Your thoughtful and insightful considerations stimulated me to clearly focus my own thoughts to bring creative solutions founded on strong bases and logic to my colleagues. Michael Novak would talk with me and not to me. He would consider my ideas and tactfully challenge my premise when necessary so I could thoroughly understand and be able to defend my positions. (That includes challenging my ELCA Lutheran pastor on occasion!) You made a substantial impact on my life and I thank God for your guidance and friendship.

Not many folks know of your love for sports and your knowledge of even the most minor details of sporting events and statistics. Your knowledge of the Dodgers has to be on par with most broadcasters today, even though you sometimes forget that Stan Musial, Enos Slaughter, Red Schoendienst and Marty Marion could also play baseball!

Sometimes your judgment is clouded by your Catholic loyalty to Notre Dame when it comes to betting on games. Whenever I look up on the wall and see the Notre Dame scarf and your Forbes article I am reminded of the score, CU 10/ ND 9. (And no, there was not a clip on that play!)

I cherish my signed copy of your book, "The Joy of Sports." When I read it from time to time I find a little more of Michael Novak, the renaissance man.

May the peace of the Lord be with you on this special day and always.

My warmest regards to my dear friend,

> *Eric Schmidt*
> *Friend*
> *Former Assistant Majority Leader, Colorado House of Representatives*
> *Former Regent, University of Colorado*
> *Former Under Secretary of Health*
> *Married to Kay Schmidt*

As a fellow octogenarian, I value memories of Michael and his contributions in many walks of life that date back to time we spent together in Rome in the mid-50's. Happy Birthday to Michael, and continued blessings in the years ahead.

> *Ernest Bartell, C.S.C. Friend*
> *Professor Emeritus of Economics*
> *Faculty Fellow, Kellogg Institute for International Studies*
> *Faculty Fellow, Institute for Educational Initiatives*
> *University of Notre Dame*

Memories of Life with Michael

My memories of Life With Michael reflect the protean quality of Michael's mind and work – which is to say, they're all over the place, even if they're finally centered on What Really Counts. So a few choice bits and pieces:

If memory serves, I was the unwitting agent of Michael's reconciliation with Richard John Neuhaus after a period of estrangement that began when Richard wrote a rather rough review of *The Rise of the Unmeltable Ethnics* in *Worldview*. Ignorant of all that, I found myself visiting Washington from what was then my base, Seattle, and Michael invited me over for dinner on Northampton Street. I guilelessly asked if I could bring along Richard, who was at the same conference I was attending; Michael agreed. Over some seriously nasty pizza aided by a bit of Scotch, while we were all sitting around the living room floor, the two discovered that they were really friends after all. And thus was born, in its mature form, the Great Catholic Neo-Con Conspiracy, the dread Novak/Neuhaus/Weigel Triumvirate, which our critics imagine to have been spawned by the Evil One before the dawn of historical time. (Connoisseurs of our tripartite friendship will be surprised to learn that the lubricant in this instance was not bourbon; that was a conversion effected later, although Michael, as a committed Manhattan man, didn't require extensive evangelization.)

As I write this in Cracow, where Michael and I spent so much time together, I can't help thinking back to our two summers in Liechtenstein, a charming if utterly boring principality, where what became the Tertio Millennio Seminar on the Free Society was born in 1992 and nourished by the hot, milky müsli in Martha Bühler's hotel breakfast room. (Martha, whose do-nothing husband used to lurk about the premises looking vaguely sinister, was the principality's most successful Olympic skier, having finished twelfth or fifteenth or something on that order in an Alpine event during the 1968 Grenoble games.) One evening, driving back from dinner at some ridiculously expensive restaurant, Michael insisted that we drive past what I remember as being Liechtenstein's only factory, which made optical lenses or some such – a digression the rest of us regarded as expressing perhaps a bit more devotion to democratic capitalism than was absolutely required. That first summer, we also visited the unfortunate Wolfgang Haas, who had been forced on the Diocese of Chur as its bishop, to which the locals did not respond, er, favorably. He gave us some dreadful white wine from the episcopal vineyards – *Swiss* wine! – and on the way back to our base at Martha Buhler's, either Richard or Michael asked me what I thought of Haas, who had become a figure of disdain to the entire global Catholic left; I said he reminded me of nothing so much as a junior Wehrmacht lieutenant on the road out of Smolensk who, when the snow began falling early in the fall of 1941, said to himself, "Oh, s**t!"

I can't remember at which lunch with John Paul II that Michael proposed that the pope make Mary Ann Glendon a cardinal, a suggestion that raised the pontifical eyebrow and led Don Stanislao (Dziwisz), master of such situations, to change the subject quickly. Perhaps it was the famous lunch right after New Year's 2000, when Michael, Karen, Joan, Richard, Maciej Zięba, and I were hosted by the pope, who, while pointing out the window of the papal dining room to the Goodyear blimp orbiting St. Peter's Square, kept saying, "You see? *Buon Anno!*" In any event, it was certainly at that memorable meal that Dziwisz asked me if "the ladies would like to see the icon," meaning the *Kazanskaya*, the literally priceless Russian crowned icon John Paul had been given, which he intended to return to Moscow, and which was kept in the papal apartment chapel. When I said that I was sure that everyone would like to see it, Dziwisz went and fetched it, handed it to me, and told me, *sotto voce*, "Explain what it is." I muttered that if I explained what it was most of those present would faint, so, without exegesis, we passed one of the four greatest expressions of Russian iconographic art around the table as if it were a box of chocolates; the explanation, later, produced something like the reaction I had predicted.

Over the course of more than three decades of friendship, it was Michael who introduced me to many things, but I think it was I who introduced him to old Memorial Stadium in Baltimore on a warm spring or summer evening in 1985 or thereabouts. One entered that great horseshoe at field level, but you couldn't see the vast greensward of the outfield until you had walked up several concrete ramps. We arrived early, as all real fans do, to watch batting practice, and as we came up the ramp and a sliver of verdant outfield came into view, a bat cracked and I said, "Greatest sound in the English language." "Except 'swish,'" Michael replied – his first and, in my presence, only dabbling with heresy.

And finally I remember the times we prayed together: in small chapels decorated with fragments of medieval fresco; in vast basilicas; saying evening prayer together in hotel rooms before proceeding on to the kind of Second Vespers distilled in Kentucky.

Never a dull moment. Never a regret about a friendship that I cherish with a man I esteem.

Ad multos gloriosque annos.

> *George Weigel*
> *Friend*
> *Author, John Paul II biography "Witness to Hope"*
> *Distinguished Senior Fellow, Ethics and Public Policy*
> *Center*

Michael at 80

Michael was born in the fall of that first year of the New Deal, when so much was in turmoil – when the regime itself would be altered, with the powers of the federal government extended in a helter-skelter way, and many people professed to find themselves in a country they no longer recognized. And so, it seems that little has changed. So many of us, in our circle, grew up as children of the New Deal and Democrats until the Second Coming of Nixon or the Advent of the Gipper. Michael marked that transition, I think, with that piece he did in the Wall Street Journal, titled something like "I'm a Closet Capitalist." He would be one of the most telling figures moving to the side of Reagan. Others would come in the circle of writers writing for Commentary magazine; they would be drawn to the Republicans on the issue of national defense. But Michael would reflect also the shift of Democrats who took seriously the issue of abortion and those so-called misnamed "social issues" – as though those moral issues running deep about life and marriage were somehow peripheral to the main business of politics.

Michael and Karen had so woven us into the life of their family – and that larger family of friends – that it's hard to recall a time when I didn't know Michael. I think I'd known him first through his pieces in *Commentary*, then the *Wall Street Journal*, and then the Washington scene, as DC became our second home in the late 70's. Michael was named as an Ambassador early in the Reagan Administration, but his standing abroad has run far more widely than anything that could be explained by an ambassadorship. His book, *The Spirit of Democratic Capitalism*, was translated into several languages, and became especially important in Eastern Europe. Years later, when I was with Michael at a seminar in Slovakia, he was invited to do a lecture at the local university, and it was a revealing sign in itself that the large lecture hall was

packed on a summer evening. Students and faculty were drawn from all parts of the University. Whether it was to recognize a Slovak who had become a world figure in letters and politics, or whether it was an audience drawn to his writings, the turnout was impressive. And it was the mark of Michael's achievement in the fuller arc of his life. He was known to that audience not only as a writer, but as a teacher of Catholicism and a gifted partisan of an American way of life.

I would speak in the series of lectures that Michael arranged at the American Enterprise Institute, but the most dramatic moment connected with AEI has to be that night at which he received that prize from AEI at a black tie dinner at the Hilton. He delivered the lecture that became the core of his book, *On Two Wings*. I can't think back to that evening without recalling Edmund Kitch, from the law school at the University of Virginia, sitting at our table, and quite transfixed as he listened to Michael unfolding the narrative in that lecture.

I began to see Michael more often when I was drawn into writing a column ("Lifewatch") for *Crisis* magazine, the journal that Michael founded with Ralph McInerny. I was recruited by my dear former student Scott Walter, who had worked for Michael before going on to his career as a writer and editor. Michael and Ralph were the most natural writers, and they had a gift for conveying orthodoxy in the most engaging way. We took that as our lead in helping to make clear anew to a Catholic audience what was truly compelling in Catholic teaching. It becomes impossible to recount or recall all of the ways in which Michael explained that teaching in lessons that were instantly graspable. And it becomes hard to recount all of the comments, funny and sage, that have been woven into these years. Michael knew that I'd been at the threshold of the Church for years, with something holding me back from taking that final step to enter. He would offer his encouragement in the gentlest way by telling Judy that he was so looking forward to sharing communion with me. And Judy would say, "He is essentially there. It's just a matter of time." When the time came, he was with me as my sponsor, and he struck off, in his characteristic way, a poem to mark the occasion.

In all of the conversations over the years he has been the most politically astute—he is never panicked by the clichés gaining the headlines of the day, and he always seems to be in touch with the sobering facts that matter. We've been disappointed, along with our other friends, over these last two elections, but he has never given up hope. And it just isn't in his makeup to quit making the arguments, the arguments that make things clearer about life and God and the way we should ever wish to be as a country. But in his large nature he saves his sanity as well by his wide range of interests with a world of sports as well as theology and politics. I recall him one night, at a Nats' game in Washington, explaining with the fascination of a theologian and a poet the importance of that distance between the pitcher's mound and home plate.

And yet, if I had a favorite story, it would be that story of a dinner at the White House in the Reagan years. He and Karen were seated opposite the legendary Lauren Bacall. Michael told her that they had seen her in *Applause,* her strikingly successful show in New York. And in a generous flourish Michael remarked that her performance had been just "marvelous." To which she said: "You'll have to do better than that, sonny." With so many years in the limelight, she was accustomed now to flattery that was routinely extravagant, offered by flatterers of world-class stature.

But in the same vein, I was thinking of the favorite jokes I retell from Michael, and I guess that I retell them because something in our politics or our lives always makes them apt in some way. One of the stories was in the familiar cast of three prisoners of war, a Frenchman, a Brit and a Russian. They are about to be executed and they are moved to wonder about the things they'd most love to do before leaving this world. The Frenchman, of course, thinks of an exquisite meal, with the right wine, and a night of love. The Brit thinks of a last meal of his favorite English fare. And the Russian? He would most savor the sight of his neighbor's barn burning down.

The other story, which I invoke far more often, is the account of the Polish Pessimist and the Optimist. The Pessimist says, "Things are dark and they can't get any worse than this." And the Optimist, ever upbeat, chimes in that "Oh, yes they can!"

It may be the sign of the times – or where we have come now as a country – that this line seems as apt and prescient as anything that might be offered in these days. But the dying Strindberg was supposed to have said, "Don't give up the argument." Michael at 80 will not give up the argument, and his friends, buoyed by his presence – and by his unfailing energy and wit as a writer – will ever stay the course with him.

> *Hadley Arkes*
> *Friend*
> *Edward N. Ney Professor of Jurisprudence and American Institutions at Amherst College*

Hi Michael,

Happy 80th Birthday!

This month while visiting my daughter in Westwood Massachusetts, I happened onto Stonehill College. I stopped for a visit and was delighted I did. The stopover brought into sharp focus the memories that you wrote about the place.

My visit with Mary Ann in April and finding Stonehill College in June awakened in me thoughts about the sleepovers with my Novak cousins when I was a boy. And the Sanders' return-visits to the various places the Novaks lived. I recall sleeping on the floor and the discussions, mostly on sports dominated by major league baseball, the St. Louis Cardinals and Stan Musial.

Although it's been almost 50 years since our last get-together face to face at Harvard, I followed your career as best I could. I was always proud to claim you as my cousin and amazed at the many people I met over the years who recognized you and were familiar with your career and writings.

As we both are now in our senior years, I sincerely hope we have another opportunity for a one-on-one discussion about our wonder years.

> *Jerry Sanders*
> *Cousin*
> *Youngest son of Mary Sanders, sister of Michael J.*
> *Novak, and George Sanders*

Michael is an American Original.

> *Ben Wattenberg*
> *Friend*
> *Author*
> *Moderator,* Think Tank

June 30, 2013

I remember Michael in Rome when we were students of theology, and he wanted to found a magazine for Holy Cross seminarians and all of the religious community. He waited with such anticipation and excitement for the first issue off the press. He knew he would be a writer, and he knew the pen was mightier than the sword.

I remember Michael at the home of St. Maria Goretti and later that day at Anzio Beach, where he was so moved by the graves of so many young Americans willing to give their lives for the freedom of others they did not know, but surely loved. He wanted to give his life for the freedom and true welfare of others world-wide, and the pen would prove mightier than the sword.

I remember Michael playing pick-up basketball with me and the brethren. He played to win. If Michael ever takes up the sword, run for your life! I thought it was just a relaxing game. Michael lived without counting the cost. He played to win the world, and the insightful written word with self-giving in many ways would characterize his life and many a memory of him.

Nicholas Ayo, c.s.c.

I remember Michael in Rome when we were students of theology, and he wanted to found a magazine for Holy Cross seminarians and all of the religious community. He waited with such anticipation and excitement for the first issue off the press. He knew he would be a writer, and he knew the pen was mightier than the sword.

I remember Michael at the home of Saint Maria Goretti and later that day at Anzio Beach, where he was so moved by the graves of so many young Americans willing to give their lives for the freedom of others they did not know, but surely loved. He wanted to give his life for the freedom and true welfare of others worldwide, and the pen would prove mightier than the sword.

I remember Michael playing pick-up basketball with me and the brethren. He played to win. If Michael ever takes up the sword, run for your life! I thought it was just a relaxing game. Michael lived without counting the cost. He played to win the world, and the insightful written word together with self-giving in many ways would characterize his life and many a memory of him.

> *Nicholas Ayo, CSC*
> *Friend*
> *Former Classmate*
> *Professor Emeritus, Program of Liberal Studies,*
> *University of Notre Dame*

Thoughts on Michael, on the Occasion of His 80th Birthday

Michael has played an enormous role in my intellectual evolution. When I was a young man I found conservatism attractive because I found his writings so attractive, in part because what Michael wrote and what he said rang so deeply true.

No one in modern times has written better on the morality of democratic capitalism and the inherent dignity of the human person. Michael's writings attracted me, and so many like me, because they were so splendidly argued, so elegantly put, and presented in such a winsome and winning manner. Michael can be tough-minded, but he is never mean-spirited. He never assumes those who disagree with him are enemies -- and unlike some on the right these days, Michael writes with the aim to persuade. And he has won over the previously unconvinced too many times to count.

Michael is, to me, a model public intellectual -- and a man of tremendous intellectual integrity.

But beyond all that, and more important than all that, is Michael's powerful, living testimony to the Lord. He loves our Savior and has devoted his mind and energy to Him and to the things He cares about. Over the course of his life Michael has done what the Lord requires of him -- to act justly and to love mercy and to walk humbly with God.

Michael will always have a special place in my mind and heart; and to count him as a friend is one of the great blessings of my life.

May his year be filled with joy and the peace of the presence of Christ.

With affection and respect,

> *Pete Wehner*
> *Friend*
> *Former Deputy Assistant to the US President*
> *Senior Fellow, Ethics and Public Policy Center*

Jana Novak and Michael Novak
TELL ME WHY
Photo credit: Karen Laub Novak

I first met Michael and Jana when I edited their jewel, *Tell Me Why,* and the experience had a profound effect on my life. Michael's quiet faith and gentle manner will stay with me always as an example of what our Catholic faith means when fully embodied in a truly good person. He is a living model for me of all I strive to be.

> *Jane Cavolina*
> *Friend*
> *Former editor, Pocket Books (imprint of Simon & Schuster Inc.)*

When I decided to launch our (Cuban) Freedom Hayek University to be set up at Guantanamo Base in Cuba, as a preamble to later move it into a future "Free Cuba," I looked for a true leader in world Freedom. I chose Michael Novak.

He not only granted me a meeting, but accepted to back my dream by becoming its Chairman. Thanks to him, I was able to meet many other world Freedom Leaders, the like of Lady Margaret Thatcher, Lech Walesa, etc. They all revered and respected Michael as their true Beacon of World Freedom.

I well remember Lady Thatcher stating Michael was her intellectual guru and ours, with Michael at its helm, a most "strategic and visionary Hemisphere freedom project to liberate the Americas of communism and indeed socialism."

Our quest was honored by fierce attacks from Fidel Castro and his liberticide accomplices, the world over. We became part of all his enemies' lists. When Lady Thatcher and Lech Walesa came to Miami to honor our Free Cubans they were firstly met by our Hayek Latin American Freedom University Chairman, my beloved friend Dr. Michael Novak.

Our tragic Cuban History, and indeed World Freedom, will never forget what this brave and lucid world leader did on our behalf! I have always felt blessed and honored by your friendship, Michael!

Happy birthday to you my transcendental and loyal friend!!

Roberto A. Weill
Friend

Founder & President, Hayek Latin American Freedom University

Lyrics to a song for Michael, when he turned…77?
(sung to the tune of "Oh What a Beautiful Mornin'")

There's a nice glass of wine on the table,

There's a martini there on the table,

The room is aboundin' with pals old and young

And it looks like you're wishin' I hadn't begun –

Oh, what a lovely evening

It was a bright autumn day

I've got a beautiful feelin'

It's Michael's birthday today.

Theologian, friend and raconteur

Much beloved by a talented painter

Handsome and witty and full of bad jokes…

But also some brilliant anec-a-dotes…

Oh, what a lovely evening

It was a bright autumn day

I've got a beautiful feelin'

It's Michael's birthday today.

Writing books without number, this Novak

Dedicated to football, this Slovak

Friend of the Pope and of the Holy See…

(An' my mortified husband is wincin' at me…)

Oh, what a lovely evening

It was a bright autumn day

I've got a beautiful feelin'

Happy birthday to Michael today.

Meghan Gurdon
Friend
Columnist

A Memory of the Wonderful Novaks!

Since I first met Karen and Michael Novak in 1980, there is a wealth of wonderful Novak memories on which to draw. Watching Karen in her studio. Visiting them at their warm, welcoming home in Washington. Meeting with Michael in his office at the American Enterprise Institute. Accompanying Karen and Michael on a lecture tour to Ireland. Listening to Michael speak on principled free enterprise in Manhattan at Pfizer, the world's largest pharmaceutical company. Confabulating about articles in *Crisis*, an intellectual magazine that Michael helped to found. Discussing Michael's work on corporate governance and intellectual property. And, of course, reading Michael's terrific books and marveling at Karen's amazing sculptures.

But my favorite memory illustrates what kind hearts Michael and Karen had. When my twin sister Maura and I were caring for our dying mother full time in Alexandria, Virginia—probably around 2003 or 2004—we invited Karen and Michael to lunch at our house. Mindful of the difficult circumstances, they came laden with gifts—most memorably, flowers so large that they obscured the person carrying them.

The Novaks were generous with their compliments about the house and the meal. After lunch, we took them upstairs to see our bed-bound mother. Although she had once spoken five languages, she then had expressive aphasia, and could not speak all. Wreathed in smiles, however, she made it clear that she was delighted to meet them and was grateful for their visit. Being an acute observer of people and also spiritually attuned to the most important things, Michael immediately recognized Mother's holiness and commented on it to us. Even so, we were totally unprepared to receive a thank you note in an envelope addressed to "The Sisters Daly and Saintly Mother." We laughed out loud when we read it and couldn't help wondering what the postman had thought!

When we showed it to our mother, she went into gales of laughter and rolled her eyes.

God bless Michael and Karen for their kind visit and for bringing so much joy into a sick room and so much consolation to those who needed it.

Carson and Maura Daly
Friends

Dr. Anne Carson Daly
Vice President of Academic Affairs, Belmont Abbey
College

Dear Michael,

Happy Birthday to a wonderful, kind and gentle friend.

Michael and I met in 1970 as Kennedy wide-eyed liberals working for "Congressional Leadership for the Future." Its goal, and our job, was to get Sargent Shriver more visibility in the Maryland Democratic Party. Shriver had returned from serving as ambassador to France one year earlier to run for Governor of Maryland. When, after a short campaign, he withdrew, his many loyal and enthusiastic supporters, of which Michael and I were two, saw "Congressional Leadership for the Future" as the best avenue for "Sarge" to move successfully into Maryland, and perhaps, national politics.

We identified races that the Democrat running had a fairly good chance of winning but needed more cash and/or press to put them over the top. The ambassador would enter the district and after a heart-warming endorsement of the candidate, the poll numbers invariably went up. Camelot was heavy in the air and Shriver's admirable lifestyle made him a great fundraiser for Democrat candidates. But the real source of his success, his strength, was the wonderful speeches Michael wrote for him that captured his thoughts in a carefully nuanced non-threatening but forceful manner. For those familiar with working for a Kennedy or a Shriver, Michael was the calm in the middle of the storm.

Peter and I were married the year Michael and I met. We consider ourselves fortunate to have him (and to have had his wonderful wife, Karen) along with Michael's sister, Mary Ann, and his brother, Ben, as our friends. Life's journey would never have been the same.

Peter, who was then, and remains, a rock solid conservative Republican, was pleased to welcome both Michael and me into his brave new world.

Happy Birthday to you, Michael.

Love,

Kathie and Peter Schaumber
Friends
Former Sargent Shriver staffers
Former Chairman and Board member, National Labor
Relations Board

Please give Michael a hearty congratulations on his birthday. My only anecdote is that in every conversation I have had with him we both beginning by telling each other how proud we are of his daughter.

> *Michael Gillespie*
> *Friend*
> *Professor of Politics, Duke University*

Nearly fifty years ago the Novaks were in Cresco visiting George and Mary. Mary Jo and I were in Cresco visiting Doc and Jo.

We got together and Michael, fresh from Berkley Commune on the left coast, and me, just back from a tough tour flying F-105s over North Vietnam, started a calm discussion of the war. The intellectual portion of our conversation ended in about one minute and we switched to less intelligent terms filled with conviction. Of course our thinking was less than accurate due to our youth. I was confident that President Johnson was trying to stem the red horde, and Michael was certain that we were all murderers that needed to listen to Jane Fonda and other leading brilliant individuals.

Well, we both were wrong. Perhaps for the right reasons, but in time we learned that our efforts in that war were without conviction and our nation was fundamentally good if we observed the faith that underscored our Constitution. I am sure we left that meeting with the conviction one of us was Joseph Stalin and the other Genghis Khan.

Then time diminished our hairline and increased our belt line, leaving us more comfortable and secure in the knowledge that the most important aspect of our lives is our families, now our children and grandchildren.

Happy Birthday Michael! We still miss Karen.

> *Chuck and Mary Jo Horner*
> *Friends*
> *Retired General, US Air Force*
> *Board of Directors, US Institute of Peace*

Michael and Karen Laub-Novak

Much of my relationship with Michael has been in the very pleasant context of shared meals – birthday dinners, casual evenings at home, and the ever-popular "I'm in town – are you free next Tuesday?" dinners. It is always a treat to spend time with Michael because of his kindness and generosity of spirit, and his vast knowledge of all things theological. I cherish the memories of relaxed meals and stimulating conversations with Michael and Karen, and I look forward to many more evening repasts with Michael – whenever he is in town!

> *Kristie Hassett*
> *Friend*
> *Wife of former American Enterprise Institute Colleague,*
> *Kevin Hassett*

Michael Novak is a prince of a man. He has saved my hide on more than one occasion (I am thinking especially of the dress code controversy!) and has made me laugh with his quick wit and good nature.

I first met him over ten years ago at Prospect House, the faculty dining hall at Princeton University. I will always remember it because I was heavily pregnant with my third child at the time. When he introduced himself to me, he said: "I'm Michael Novak. It is nice to meet you. And thank you for doing your part to save Social Security."

Michael Novak and I became much closer after I left Princeton to work at Ave Maria University. In those early years at the temporary campus, when money was plentiful but faculty morale was not, he made a point of meeting with faculty members to hear their perspectives and let them know that there was at least one University trustee who took their concerns seriously. As a result of his advocacy on behalf of the faculty, many struggling Catholic families benefited from much needed salary increases and greater housing security, which went very far to bolstering morale until the institution was finally accredited.

I have had the privilege of listening to him give several formal lectures and I have even participated in a few panel discussions with him. He is wise and accessible, fighting for liberty and virtue with good humor and charming anecdotes, always remembering that the key to making a connection with your audience is to love them.

I have also had the privilege of sharing more than one meal with him and of talking with him as his friend about whatever happens to enter his mind. Usually, his beloved Karen is on his mind. Michael Novak has a romantic streak. He loves women, and has said to me on more than one occasion that he believes women have richer interior lives than men. Karen is with him all the time, and it is her interior life that occupies his heart and soul. Somehow I suspect that especially in the wee hours of the morning when all is silent, he is thinking of her.

Michael Novak is wise and loveable. Students love him. Scholars at Ave Maria University love him. Anyone who takes the time to get to know him cannot help but love him. I am incredibly fortunate to be able to call this man my friend. I love him, too.

Thank you, Michael.

Have a very happy 80th birthday! Thank you for making this world a much happier place to be in.

Your friend and admirer,

> *Seana Sugrue*
> *Friend*
> *Professor of Political Economy and Government, Ave Maria University*

I first encountered Michael Novak the way most people did, through his books. I read the *Spirit of Democratic Capitalism* as soon as it came out; at the time, we were all still trying to get used to the reality of Reagan's improbably huge victory. There it was: in his book, Michael had captured perfectly the nation's unique vision of freedom and self-reliance, a vision at once religious and practical. Quite a feat, though he made it look easy. I was sure the man himself was larger than life.

It wouldn't be long till my husband and I finally did meet Michael in person, along with his equally charming wife Karen. His formidable prose notwithstanding, Michael himself turned out to be humble and affectionate, endowed with a capacity for listening rare in an academic, and an unmistakable twinkle in his eye. His warmth was instantaneous, and overwhelming.

Over the years, that impression was reconfirmed, again and again. His capacity for intimacy and his unaffected generosity of soul never failed to surprise me. He would radiate affection as few people can, and fewer do.

Then a few years ago, I told Michael about the book I was writing, entitled *Soulmates: Resurrecting Eve*, which focuses on the centrality of mutual respect among human beings, as illustrated in the narrative of Adam and Eve. The message of that story is common to all three of the Abrahamic religions (which, parenthetically, took misogynist turns, albeit in various directions and intensities). Little did I know that Michael's own discussion of *caritas* captured very much the same idea – which I gratefully used in my book, to help clarify my argument.

But it is one thing to demonstrate intellectually that spiritual equality among all of God's children is central to our civilization and quite another to inspire fallible, selfish human beings to act decently. For the spirit of democratic capitalism to bind our hearts, it must touch the core of our being. Michael Novak not only articulated the concept, he showed us what it means: he gave us his love.

> *Juliana Geran Pilon, Ph.D*
> *Friend*
> *Faculty Chairman*
> *Director, Center for Culture and Security, Institute of World Politics*

My friend Michael,

You are one of God's great men, and I prize and treasure our friendship more than words can say.

Your life has been a testament of faith, hope, and charity, and when God made you brilliant, He also made you compassionate and full of light and life.

May the years ahead be ones of wonder and blessings and joy in Him.

Tim Goeglein
Friend
Vice President for External Relations, Focus on the Family

Dear Michael,

On the occasion of your 80th birthday, I want to write you this personal letter to wish you a most happy and holy birthday, and to thank you.

Michael, I also want to express in this letter some thoughts that I have possessed for several years, which I have not yet communicated to you.

In January of 2003, when I was serving as U.S. Ambassador to the Holy See, and the Holy Father at the Annual Diplomatic Reception looked straight at me and said, "No to war!", meaning, in no uncertain terms, that he did not think the United States should invade Iraq, I turned immediately to my trusted friend, Michael Novak, and called you to discuss this situation and to ask for your help.

One of the reasons I did that was that you were (and are) one of the most respected American laymen in the Vatican. They knew you; they knew your intelligence, your integrity and your character. Also, not least on my part, was the fact that you had a very close personal relationship with the Pope. Or as they say in Rome: "You had great access to the Papal Apartment." This latter point is important because you were good friends with the Pope, and yet you risked hurting that relationship by taking a public position, in Italy no less, strongly opposite to that of your friend, the Pope John Paul II.

The first thing you said to me on my call was that you agreed with President Bush's position, i.e. that it was both necessary for us to go into Iraq to disrupt Saddam Hussein and his intentions to hurt the United States of America, and that it was moral to do so.

Then I asked if there was any way that you could come to Rome and speak to various audiences there about both the righteousness of the U.S. position and its morality. You said you were in the middle of a hectic schedule, but because I asked, and because of the importance of the situation, that you would come to Rome immediately. You did just that.

This was an act of considerable courage and character, and one that you could easily have passed on. But you didn't, because you are who you are – an extraordinary man of competence, compassion, and principle, and a great patriot.

Your appearances in Rome were attended by thousands, and your help was invaluable in explaining the U.S. position to the Vatican, to Italy, to the EU, and their respective press corps.

You did all of this at a moment's notice and while risking one of the most important and cherished relationships that you had developed in your lifetime.

You did, Michael, what your whole life has epitomized – you did the right thing. It was very helpful to me, the President's principal interlocutor with the Pope, and I am eternally grateful and respectful.

Suzanne joins me in sending you our warmest birthday greetings, and our prayers for your continued good health and welfare. God Bless You.

Sincerely yours,

> *Jim Nicholson*
> *Friend*
> *Former Ambassador to the Vatican*
> *Former Secretary of Veterans Affairs*

I did not know Michael well, but I think of him as a lovely, gentle, immensely thoughtful man, who was willing to talk about deeply personal matters in a remarkably open way. I always loved talking to him.

> *Abigail Thernstrom*
> *Political Scientist*
> *Vice Chair of the United States Commission on Civil Rights*

Regarding Michael Novak, I heard him speak a couple of years ago and I brought over his book *Washington's God* for him to autograph. He is such a kind man and his face lit up when I mentioned that I had been in contact with his daughter. Their book, *Washington's God*, strongly influenced my views on my favorite historical figure, George Washington. He is one of the few scholars I have read to stand up firmly for the evidence that Washington was a devout man - not the anticlerical Deist he has been made to be by modern scholars. It was clear, during the event, that Dr. Novak is a man of great wisdom and insight, and the audience came away edified by his keen mind and sharp wit.

> *Richard Lim*
> *Friend*
> *Student*

My recollections of Michael and Karen are many. I recall reading Michael's books, some with Karen's illustrative art, and being so pleased to meet them both at St. Leo's Abbey when they came to a Conference on Lonergan's work in 1970. In the decades since that first meeting I followed Michael in his stellar career, meeting him at the American Enterprise Institute and rejoicing with all his many friends when his epoch-making *The Spirit of Democratic Capitalism* contributed to his winning the Templeton Prize in 1994.

It is a special joy to have both Michael and his brother, Ben, living here in Ave Maria. The students and visitors enjoy his seminars and lectures, and especially the evenings at the Queen Mary Pub when Michael will regale the packed audience with the many recollections of his many friends, each of whom he knew in their unique personalities and gifts: from popes, prime ministers, and business leaders to neighbors, workers, waitresses, and acquaintances. All he could recount with verve and humor as illustrations of the great procession of humanity towards eternal life in the communion of saints with the Father, Son, and Holy Spirit.

Here is a small occasion that illustrates Michael's wonderful insight and sense of humor. An assistant of his expressed interest in doing a graduate degree in Theology here at Ave Maria University. Michael told him to contact me. Later Michael came down and asked if I had heard from him. I said not yet. When Michael went back to Washington, DC, and then AEI, he asked the assistant if he had in the meantime contacted me. The young man said: "No, I cannot go this year." To this Michael immediately replied: "What's her name?"

With prayers of thanksgiving for all that Michael, Karen, and their wonderful family have contributed to the fun, enlightenment, and grace of our human pilgrimage.

> *Rev. Matthew Lamb*
> *Friend*
> *Professor of Theology, Ave Maria University*

If I had time I could tell you quite a few stores on Michael and on a group of friends in the late eighties and early nineties, with George Weigel, Richard Neuhaus and others. But since I have a short time I must select only one story, of which Michael was the subject although he was not present there.

Perhaps you know that in the eighties Michael was a very controversial figure in public discussion in the United States and also in the United States Church. There had been a letter of the American bishops on the moral issues connected to the possession of nuclear weapons. Michael together with his friends had written an answer to this letter defending the right of the United States to posses these weapons within a strategy of defense of their vital national interest and of liberty in the world.

There was a heated debate in the Vatican too, because somebody wanted, one way or another, a word of the Pope against Michael Novak to settle the question. *Roma locuta causa finita.* John Paul II wanted me to tell him what I thought of Michael Novak and of the accusations made against him. I was very prudent, as one has to be when he speaks to the Holy Father. I had read most of the books of Michael's, but I did not want to take the responsibility of a clear cut answer. So I started arguing more or less like this: this is good; this is less good; this may justify the criticisms, this seems to contradict them ... Then I did not know Michael personally. I had seen him a couple of times but it was too little to say that I did know him. In the end the Holy Father, who had a keen sense of humor, concluded: "Novak.....it is a Slovak name, he cannot be thoroughly bad. I want to see him." The rest of the story Michael can tell you himself. I only know is that they became friends and John Paul II was happy to see him whenever he could.

All my best wishes for Michael's birthday. He is a good friend.

With my best greetings,

> *Rocco Buttiglione*
> *Friend*
> *Professor of Political Science*
> *Saint Pius V University in Rome*
> *Member, Pontifical Academy of Social Sciences*

More than forty years ago, I first discovered articles by and about Michael Novak (possibly his column in *National Review?)* and knew that this was a man of ideas that I wanted to know more about. Over the years, I read his books and articles and even photocopied every article by and about him, which I still possess to this day.

In 1974, I contacted ISI (Intercollegiate Studies Institute) about bringing their weeklong seminar for schoolteachers called *The Role of Business in Society* (ROBIS) to Colorado. As a former teacher, I had visited their ROBIS program at Stanford University and was impressed with its intellectual vigor. After obtaining funding to bring the program to the University of Colorado, I knew that Michael Novak was the perfect speaker to end the program with an inspiring conclusion. Michael was warmly received by teachers as well as business leaders who funded the program. In fact, they stayed 45 minutes afterward for questions & answers. This was the beginning of a deep respect and growing friendship with Michael on the part of my husband, Eric and me.

Soon after this, I was asked to be the President of the *Colorado Council on Economic Education* (CCEE) whose mission it was to promote economic education for teachers throughout Colorado. As I accepted the challenge, I began work with local professors of Economics to design & implement programs for all levels of teachers (K-12). I always kept Michael in mind for instances where his unique knowledge of economics and the free society would benefit our teachers.

Some years later, we initiated an *Economics for Clergy* program, which we conducted for almost a decade. A weekend program in Vail with a complement of economics professors who provided a basic understanding of economics combined with Michael's theological expertise resulted in an inspiring and "eye-opening" program for Colorado clergy. Michael will remember many of the fine University faculty, including Dr. Paul Ballantyne, Dr. Timothy Tregarthen and Dr. Barry Poulson, with whom he collaborated. The clergy were so intrigued that many asked to return to enhance their new knowledge. One of the great testaments for the influence of this program came from my own pastor, Dr. Luther Bergland, who said that the program became a "life-changing" experience for him. When Pastor Bergland retired from his ministry at Atonement Lutheran Church in Boulder, the congregation asked him what he might enjoy as a retirement gift. Without hesitation, he asked them to bring Michael Novak to Boulder to do a series of events at the University and at his congregation. What a tribute to Michael Novak!

During my tenure as CCEE President, one of my favorite programs, which provided outreach to a wider community, was an annual lecture series which was begun with a grant from the Scholl Foundation and later funded by the Templeton Foundation in addition to other Colorado donors, including Terry Considine. We were fortunate to bring to Colorado some of American's most distinguished intellectuals, including: Charles Murray, American Enterprise Institute; Thomas Sowell, Hoover Institution at Stanford; Victor Davis Hanson, Hoover Institution; Murray Weidenbaum, Center for the Study of Business at St. Louis University; Lord Peter Bauer, London School of Economics; British historian, Paul Johnson; Steve Forbes, *Forbes* Magazine; and of course, Michael Novak, American Enterprise Institute.

Over more than two decades, Michael came to Colorado as a guest speaker, at least once a year, and occasionally several times. After that, Michael often teased me that I was helping him put his children through college by way of his Colorado honorarium.

One of the most treasured moments of our life concerning Michael Novak was the opportunity for Eric and me to travel to London for the awarding of the prestigious *Templeton Prize for Progress in Religion.*

Because we arrived early for the reception, following his award from the Queen at Buckingham Palace, which was held at the Oxford-Cambridge Club, Eric and I had the experience of speaking with Sir John Templeton privately for at least 20 to 30 minutes. What a thrill to meet the man who originated the *Templeton Award in Religion*, which was meant to rival the Nobel Prize awards.

After the award, it was a great honor for Eric and me to be invited to a private dinner at the Savoy in London with Michael and Karen, their family members and several other Americans who came to London for this momentous occasion.

Michael's address in Westminster Abbey as recipient of the *Templeton Award* was the thrill of a lifetime, and we will never forget that Margaret Thatcher, members of Parliament, and royalty attended the inspiring ceremony.

The Spirit of Democratic Capitalism is my favorite Novak book and I have introduced many people to this great work, which changed the world and influenced the Solidarity Movement in Poland as well as the Pope, Presidents, and Prime Ministers. I have never passed up an opportunity to introduce friends, acquaintances, and others to this monumental work.

Over the years we were privileged to have Michael and Karen stay in our home on numerous occasions and to visit their lovely ocean residence in Lewes, Delaware, as well as their home in Washington, D.C. We have also enjoyed knowing extended members of the family like Jana, Mary Ann, Ben and others.

We love and cherish Michael and what his friendship has meant to us, as well as how his intellect has enriched our lives and furthered the knowledge of all who know his work. We wish him a very Happy Birthday on the momentous occasion of his 80th.

> *Kay Schmidt*
> *Friend*
> *Former president, Colorado Center for Economic*
> *Freedom*
> *Married to Eric Schmidt*

It has always been surprising to me in conversation with Michael Novak – his voice and tone are so soft, so gentle and so forbearing it is almost inappropriate when considering the importance of what he has to say.

He has the remarkable and insightful capability to help one find profound new meaning in most everything, be it a stone, a gate post or God Himself.

Life is a gift. So is Michael. Happy Birthday.

> *Charles Carroll Carter*
> *Friend*
> *Descendant of one of the Founding Families of the United*
> *States (Charles Carroll signed the Declaration of*
> *Independence)*

Dear Michael,

Happy Birthday! With your devoted family and legion of friends –
can I include myself among them? – I praise God for your eight
decades, and entrust the future years, many and vigorous, I pray,
into the hands of Jesus through Mary.

Pardon me for bringing this up, but, more than any of your
splendid books, articles, and talks, I was most moved by your
tender, faithful love for Karen, especially in her illness. The two
of you were, for me, what married couples are called to be by that
sacrament: an icon of God's love for us. Thanks!

Wish I were with you!

Faithfully,

> *+Timothy Michael Cardinal Dolan*
> *Friend*
> *Archbishop of New York*

Though I really do not know Michael in person, the few times we
corresponded on email showed me that he has a compassionate
heart. I am grateful that you have him as your friend & if God
wishes maybe I will meet him one day.

I appreciate all the help he extended to me! God bless you.

> *Josephine Adubango*
> *Former of student of David Burrell, CSC*

My husband and I had the joy of getting to know Michael when we were at Ave Maria University, my husband as a grad student and Michael's assistant, and I a fundraiser.

There are two memories that stand out distinctly from our time with Ambassador, who always told us to just call him Michael. The first is from our many "dinner-and-a-movie dates" at his condo. He'd frequently ask us to join him for dinner, which usually meant cocktails (he introduced me, serendipitously, to the Manhattan!), then a pasta dinner, and a musical on DVD. I think at least two or three times we watched South Pacific in its entirety, and that's a three-plus hour film! Michael would sit on his chair and sing along to every song, and always had new information for us, tidbits of cultural or time-appropriate notes, no matter how many times we watched. On one such evening, noting that I'd had two Manhattans, he told me I'd better stop. He shared his favorite poem with me, next:

> I like to have a martini
>
> Two at the very most
>
> After three I'm under the table
>
> After four I'm under my host!

My second memory is that of Michael's attendance at our wedding. I grew up in a very rural town about two hours outside of Pittsburgh. To get there, Michael had to travel from Florida to Pittsburgh, have my brother (a stranger to Michael) drive him two hours home, and stay in a less-than-luxurious hotel for a few nights. We invited him, hoping he'd come, but sure that it was too much to ask of our important friend. But he came, and he was there for every part of the event, from the rehearsal to family photos and the ceremony itself. For my husband and me, who have no living grandparents, it was truly a delight to have our friend Michael present, particularly because we had heard so much from him about his wonderful wife Karen, whom we never had the joy of meeting.

Thanks, and Happy Birthday to our dear friend Michael.

> *Amy and Harrison Garlick*
> *Friends*
> *Ave Maria University students and staff*

Dear Michael,

This project gave Bill and me an opportunity to recall many fond memories of the times you and your family visited us on the way to and from Boston, where you and your brothers were attending school. My family looked forward to those visits since we had so few cousins in Conn. and you all brought much fun, information, and new perspectives.

At that time, we were so immersed in child rearing and care of parents that we were out of touch with the wider world. Long conversations with you all helped us to understand our family history, and how our parents and your grandparents as immigrants faced the challenges of assimilating into the culture of a new country.

You also brought a new awareness of world events, politics and religion, especially the role of the missionaries in the Church.

In the spirit of our Church's ministry to the poor, Bill and I have made a donation to the Farmworkers Community Center in Immokalee, Fla. This center will serve the thousands of workers who labor in the fields nearby. It will provide space to hold weekly meetings, and a radio station and make computers and media equipment available so that these workers can reap the benefits of the information age.

So, my dear cousin, may you have a blessed, happy birthday and enjoy many more to come.

Much love,

> *Irene and Bill O'Day*
> *Cousins*

It was thirty years ago, when my wife, Brenda, and I were attending a conference of the Young Presidents Organization in Copenhagen, Denmark, that we met Michael. Over three consecutive days he presented his treatise on Democratic Capitalism. I was mesmerized. I heard a message that resonated with what I knew were the components of creating freedom and realizing its benefits. It was so clear and so complete! Shortly thereafter, Michael presented the opportunity to support his work. It was the beginning of a long-term journey of admiration coupled with friendship that has been so very meaningful to me.

Thank you Michael, and God Bless,

> *Joe Calihan*
> *Friend*
> *Managing Partner, Bradford Capital Partners*
> *Director Emeritus, The Pittsburgh Foundation*

We are so grateful to have met Michael Novak in 2005! Ever since we have become friends and spent memorable times together with both Michael and Karen, those treasured moments are always present in our hearts. Michael has been instrumental in, and a source of inspirational ideas for, a number of my paintings and notably the new portrait of George Washington, which is today in the permanent collection of the Mount Vernon museum.

His wisdom, knowledge, and theological foundation have guided me in every single encounter, whether in conversations or emails. He is soft spoken and always to the point, with a great sense of humor, earthy and humble, and a leader of men in his spiritual core of values. He will always remain my mentor in many ways.

Mary refers to Michael as the C. S. Lewis of Catholicism and several of his books and poems have had special significance in her life of faith and family. She proudly brought one of his newly published books to the Vatican as a gift to Pope Benedict XVI, who was thrilled to receive it and excited to remark that His Holiness was a great fan and had read all his books!

Mary, Michael and Carole recently spent a magical evening together at dinner in Naples at a favorite Italian restaurant, entertaining the guests with a medley of songs and ballads, and had a grand ole time! We are blessed to know this extraordinary man and that our paths have crossed in this beautiful journey of life.

We love you Michael, and wish you a very happy birthday!

> *Igor Babailov and Mary Calia Babailov*
> *Friend*
> *American Portrait Artist*
> *Honorary Academician of the Russian Academy of Arts*

When I think of Michael Novak, I smile.

Truly – I just smile and feel happy.

Somewhere in a pop psychology article I once read that the only thing we really recall about the individuals we have known in life is how they made us feel.

So that tells you something right off the bat.

If thinking about Michael Novak makes me happy, it's not just because he made me laugh (though he often did), or offered an amusing observation on a tricky situation –whether it be social, political, or economic. It's that, along with the humor came great wisdom. And I don't mean of the pontifical variety; with Michael, the wisdom is delivered with a sense of understanding, appreciation and affection for humans and their foibles. He seems to have a special insight into what we all might be capable of doing, what we all, and each individually, might aspire to achieve.

I first became aware of Michael Novak when I heard Jack Kemp extolling *The Spirit of Democratic Capitalism* as a brilliant work destined to be a classic. Of course, I had to read it immediately. And through my slow grasping of Novak's carefully-developed and logical arguments, I came to recognize the theological connection between self-government and free markets, the morality of free will and free enterprise.

What a gift.

Michael provided an intellectual wellspring that proved liberating for me, justifying the innate righteousness of economic freedom not only as the most appropriate and beneficial system for a free society, but as the key to individual empowerment and fulfillment. Instead of having to step around the notion of greed, Michael helped me understand that the ideals of charity, trust and cooperation are best achieved through economic growth, liberty and opportunity. Entrepreneurial endeavor unleashes our most admirable human traits.

He was the famous "Michael Novak" to me then, successful author and genius philosopher. It would be years later before I actually met the man. And though he still remains a genius to me, he is also my friend forever. And he is revered on both counts.

Michael, do you remember one time, at a Super Bowl confab that took place in the late nineties, we were talking quietly together and I suddenly blurted out that I might want to try to write something – just for myself – on what I believed with regard to Christ? No one would have guessed, I suppose, that an economic policy wonk more associated with global finance and monetary issues had a burning desire to try to figure out what my faith was based on. But you didn't seem the least bit fazed by this confession of mine. You nodded and went thoughtfully silent a few moments. Then you looked at me with that expression of yours – I can still picture those earnest eyes that convey warmhearted honesty and caring –

and in a gentle voice you told me that it was a fine idea.

"But it's not something that would ever be published, " came my protesting response, even though my heart was beating faster at the realization that you took my plan seriously and even supported it.

"Doesn't matter whether you publish it or not," you stated calmly. "Even if you work on it with diligence and devotion, and then put it away forever in a desk drawer, it will still have been worth your full attention and sincere effort."

I think I managed to whisper "thank you" and then turned away before you could quite make out my tears of happiness and relief. Somehow I had long been afraid to commit myself to a project so at odds with my own sense of "professionalism" and worldly accomplishment. But you gave me that freedom to explore my own religious convictions.

And I did write that book for myself. It took more than two years. And you were right: The personal effort was well worth it. The endeavor has made a huge difference in my life, my values. It brought Gil and me to Israel and other locales as part of the spiritual journey. It has made everything on earth more meaningful because it enabled my heart and soul to link this whole experience to a greater eternity.

And guess what – I'm smiling right now.

Thinking of you.

With deep admiration and affection and gratitude,

Judy Shelton
Friend
Author and Economist
Co-Director, Sound Money Project at the Atlas Economic
Research Foundation
Wife of Gil Shelton

Michael has accomplished more in just ONE of his eight decades than most people accomplish in ALL of their decades.

One of the works I appreciate most is his collaboration with his daughter, Jana. Their book, *Washington's God: Religion, Liberty, and the Father of Our Country,* is a fascinating historical account. In his own way, Michael ended the debate - clarifying once and for all that Washington's God was that of Abraham, Isaac and Jacob.

We are eternally grateful for the heart and the spirit of Michael. May this 80th year be one of many blessings!

God bless.

> *Alan Sears*
> *Friend*
> *President, CEO & General Counsel, Alliance Defending*
> *Freedom*

Though Michael's and my life diverged before long, we were joined at the hip in Rome with Bernard Lonergan, our esteemed mentor.

Yet we have recently recovered our friendship as "emeriti," a great title. Intervening years – "professional ones," if you will – found us at odds politically.

Indeed, the earlier friendship made those years of separation even more painful, for I felt we no longer shared the Aristotelian circle of "the good."

The one who brought us back together, of course, is the same one who kept us united despite everything – Karen.

Thrown together at a gala dinner in D.C. a few years ago, along with Cardinal Scola, I spent the time with Karen, catching up on family.

So when Karen died, we needed to let her fresh presence bring us together.

I could then confess to him that I had "passed judgment" on him during the AEI years, unable to read his stuff. But judgment is never acceptable.

So we found our way back together, testily, of course, as men caught in sibling rivalry must always do! Yet once each could confess to be prodigals, we could proceed!

I have always felt a special connection to Michael and to Mary Ann, via Richard, whom I had met only once, but whose spirit hovers over this land.

Last month, March 1 and 2, Dick Timm and I each celebrated a milestone: Dick 90 years, and I, 80. How grand to feel 80 years young!

Most recently, Michael and I have conspired to help a former student, Josephine Adubango, with her child Eliana, to a fresh start in Istanbul.

For this above all, and for other recent reminders, I have given thanks to God for bringing us together and for the Lord's care for us in our lives.

> *David Burrell, CSC*
> *Friend*
> *Former Classmate*

There are so many personal anecdotes – a long, cold, and fun ball game at Camden Yards and a spectacular 60th birthday dinner at Jean-Louis come to mind.

But at the top of the list is a casual conversation in the halls of AEI when I was beginning work on *Human Accomplishment.* As we talked about the daunting assignment I had given myself, Michael said quietly that the further I got into the story of the Renaissance and thereafter, the more pivotal I would find Christianity's role to be. I privately doubted it, but his words never left me, and they opened my mind to possibilities, which, five years later, led me to write that: "The Greeks laid the foundation, but it was the transmutation of that foundation by Christianity that gave modern Europe its impetus and differentiated European accomplishment from that of all other cultures around the world."

I have since wondered how *Human Accomplishment* would have been diminished if not for Michael's gentle words in that short conversation.

Happy birthday, Michael. And thanks.

> *Charles Murray*
> *Friend*
> *American libertarian political scientist and author*
> *Fellow at American Enterprise Institute*

Here are a few of my favorite memories from working in the "God corner" with Michael:

1) At the end of my first week on the job, Michael took me, Jana, and our intern Matt to an Orioles-Dodgers game at Camden Yards.

We had parked in a nearby garage and were headed toward the ballpark. Michael started walking really quickly and ended up getting about a block ahead of us. Jana turned to me and said: "He'll probably get to the gate before he realizes we're not with him." It was the first instance I can remember of the single-minded, almost tireless focus he could bring to whatever he wanted, be it a new column, a new book, or getting to the ballpark on time!

2) I was often amazed at how I could draft correspondence and other documents for him and when he edited those documents, instead of re-writing some passages, he would re-arrange my own words in a way he preferred. I learned so much about using language when I worked for him. I also became much more adept at reading difficult handwriting!

3) I loved our Blue Bunny ice cream party ritual for departing interns.

4) I also loved how quietly generous he could be with people, especially those who were relative strangers.

5) When I saw he had written a book on theology and the "joy of sports," I knew I wanted to work for this man.

6) "Krakow Surprise":

I began working for Michael Novak on September 11, 2001, which also happened to be the day after Julie and I returned from our honeymoon. After the Slovak Seminar the following July, Michael, Russ Hittinger, Roman Karabelli and I were making our way from Slovakia to Krakow for the Tertio Millennio Institute. Little did I know but Julie and Michael had hatched a plot to surprise me. Working as a consultant for Deloitte at the time, Julie had a business trip to South Africa and arranged to stop in Krakow for the first weekend of the Institute.

As we approached the center of Krakow, Michael said that my room in the monastery, where the other students were staying, was not ready, and that I would be staying in a hotel for a couple of nights. It seemed a little odd that they could not find *somewhere* in the monastery to put me, but after all the work of organizing the Slovak Seminar, a couple of nights in a hotel sounded great, so without thinking too much about it, I said okay.

I think Roman must have led me into the hotel. He gave the front desk lady my name, and, nervously, she looked up my room number. The bellhop led me up to the room. I opened the door, stepped in, and noticed a woman's jacket draped over a chair. Thinking that the front desk must have made a mistake, I turned around and walked out of the room. The bellhop must not have been in on the joke because he looked really confused. Then I heard a woman's voice behind me say "Grattan." I turned around and there she was! Julie, who was supposed to be in South Africa! It all made sense . . . the hotel, the odd front desk clerk, and the confused bellman.

Julie and I had a terrific few days together in Krakow. Julie especially loved the opening lectures of the seminar and getting to know the other participants. Thanks for making it happen, Michael!

Happy Birthday!

> *Grattan Brown*
> *Friend*
> *Former assistant to Michael*
> *Assistant Professor of Theology, Belmont Abbey College*

I have one funny little story:

Michael got a "sneak peak" at the manuscript for my book, *"In the Hands of a Good Providence": Religion in the Life of George Washington*, while he and his daughter were working on their own book, *Washington's God*. He was kind enough to write a blurb for my book, even before there was a publisher for it, and was always very supportive.

When my book finally came out, Michael and Jana were at the top of the invitation list for a presentation I was giving about the process of researching and writing it for my bosses, the Mount Vernon Ladies' Association, during their Fall Council in 2008. Jana was off getting married or something, but Michael and Karen both came and he insisted on preceding me onstage to give an introduction. I was waiting in the wings for the right moment to make my entrance, so I got to hear what your dad had to say, which was very kind. When I came out, I got a hug, and he went to take his seat beside Karen in the first row.

And then I really got going. One of the problems with being an introvert, who spends most of her time researching people who've been dead for more than 150 years, is that when you do get the chance to stand in front of an audience with a microphone, there is a tendency to let loose. And I did. Afterwards, people who had known me for years said, "I never knew you were so funny!"

Unfortunately, one major slip-up came when I got to the part of the talk where I discussed recent works on the topic of Washington and religion, which had been of help in one way or another. Of course, I mentioned *Washington's God*, because Michael and Jana had answered the Washington as a deist question so well that I didn't have to fight that particular battle in my book.

So, with my mouth on auto-pilot, I said that I owed a great debt to Robert Novak and his daughter for having written that fantastic book. The Regent of the Mount Vernon Ladies' Association, Gay Hart Gaines, was sitting in the middle of the front row and said, "No, it was Michael Novak." I stopped my talk and leaned down to talk to her for a second, because I didn't really hear her the first time. So, then I heard what I'd said and wanted to sink through the stage floor, and said something like, "Oh no, and I know the difference!" The mike picked up all of this, so the audience, which included your parents, who were sitting next to Mrs. Gaines, was rolling on the floor.

I picked up where I'd left off and the rest of the talk went well, with no bloopers. Later, as I was signing books, Michael and Karen came up to have me sign a copy for Jana, and I profusely apologized for crediting Robert Novak with writing *Washington's God*. Michael was very sweet about it, and Karen busted up again.

At least I wasn't on BookTV or something when it happened!

Give Michael a big hug for me on his birthday!

> *Mary V. Thompson*
> *Friend*
> *Research Historian, Mount Vernon Estates & Garden*

"The Theology of Capitalism"

One of Michael's visits to Bangladesh took place while his brother Jim resided here as Director of the Asia Foundation in Bangladesh. He probably was instrumental in having Michael invited by the leading economists of Bangladesh to give them a talk on *The Spirit of Democratic Capitalism*.

About a week in advance of the talk I had a phone call from Professor Rehman Sobhan, the Chairman for the occasion. He said they had heard that Michael would include something in his talk about the theology of capitalism, and he was afraid that everyone might be mystified and the subject might be too abstruse for them. I laughed and said that he would surely speak in such a way that everyone could clearly understand him. He wanted more reassurance than that and asked me to be present to act as a kind of theological interpreter, if necessary. I willingly assented and showed up at the proper time.

The gathering was held on the top floor of the Sonargaon Hotel, Dhaka's only five-star hotel, in the Lecture Room. A big crowd was present, and Michael quickly put them at ease with his clear-cut explanations of his main ideas. It was only toward the end that he brought up the subject of theology. He began in a simple way, explaining how we are all inter-related through the first man and woman, Adam and Eve. He used the expression from the Book of Genesis: "We are all made in the image of the same God."

That was heresy to one of my good friends, who leaped to his feet and cried out: "No, no, you cannot say that. God is so far above all of us that we cannot share in his image." I did not feel that my intervention was called for at that point. In fact, I was anxious to see how Michael would deal with the answer. Michael did not want to provoke controversy, so he skillfully backed out of any discussion at all about the theology of capitalism.

It was only later that I learned that almost the exact wording that Michael used from Genesis is found in the Quran! I would have loved to have been able to quote this at the time as a lesson in tolerance but I was not up to the mark as a faithful theological interpreter.

> *Rev. Fr. Richard W. Timm, CSC*
> *Friend of the Family*

The poem to the right reminded me not only of the complexity of
parenting, but of Karen's archer. It seemed fitting as a tribute for
the gifts you both gave your children. Not knowing where the
arrows may land, or fly, at least they were sprung from a stable
place. Richard and I are grateful for your many examples of
wisdom, kindness and laughter – yes! the best is last. That talent
for humor is only bested by the spirit of humility behind it. It has
been a humbling and heart-warming experience. The grace you
brought to the world is priceless. Many thanks forever!

With our love,
Richard and Lucy Novak
Son and Daughter-in-law

"Children"
by Kahlil Gibran (the Prophet)

Your children are not your children.
They are the sons and daughters of Life's longing for itself.
They come through you but not from you,
And though they are with you yet they belong not to you.

You may give them your love but not your thoughts,
For they have their own thoughts.
You may house their bodies but not their souls,
For their souls dwell in the house of tomorrow,
Which you cannot visit, not even in your dreams.
You may strive to be like them,
But seek not to make them like you.
For life goes not backward nor tarries with yesterday.

You are the bows from which your children
As living arrows are sent forth.
The archer sees the mark upon the path of the infinite,
And He bends you with His might
That His arrows may go swift and far.
Let your bending in the archer's hand be for gladness;
For even as He loves the arrow that flies,
So He loves also the bow that is stable.

ABOUT THE AUTHORS

Jana Novak is Michael's youngest child;
Alston Novak is his eldest grandchild.

Printed in Great Britain
by Amazon

71816770R10067